# *130*
# CHICKEN NUGGETS

# *130* CHICKEN NUGGETS

*A Breakup in Verse*

MERCEDEZ FERNANDEZ

 iUniverse®

**130 CHICKEN NUGGETS**
**A BREAKUP IN VERSE**

*Illustrated by: Aira San Agustin*

*iUniverse books may be ordered through booksellers or by contacting:*

*iUniverse*
*1663 Liberty Drive*
*Bloomington, IN 47403*
*www.iuniverse.com*
*1-800-Authors (1-800-288-4677)*

*ISBN: 978-1-5320-7405-9 (sc)*
*ISBN: 978-1-5320-7406-6 (e)*

*Library of Congress Control Number: 2019905189*

*Print information available on the last page.*

*iUniverse rev. date: 04/26/2019*

Dedicated to: Mr. Dodt,
Who taught me logic, philosophy, history, and poetry–
Basically all you really need to know.

Before my best friend moved to Utah,
we would lie on her trampoline and look at the stars,
picking out constellations, researching timeless Greek
legends,
creating our own stories, painting our own lines across
the sky,

the sky that was one big game of connect the dots,
featuring Ursa Minor, Orion, Scorpius—
Scorpius, who fell only to rise with offspring,
climbing, inching, closer, closer.
Scorpions on the walls,

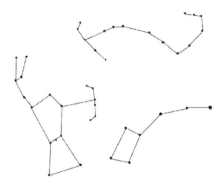

prompting high-pitched shrieks and thrown snacks—
blueberries, chips, chicken nuggets—
as if the dinosaur-shaped bites in all their might, glory,
and wisdom
would protect us from the arachnoids.

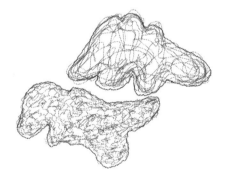

You know, I was never really a fan of scorpions. Come to think of it, is anyone a fan of scorpions, except for maybe, well, scorpions?

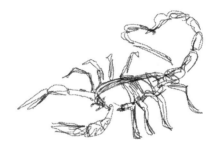

I was always more of a butterfly kind of gal.
Maybe it's because of my mother,
or maybe it's because of the caterpillar I raised at eight years old.
I remember holding the mason jar in the back seat of the minivan,
steadying the chrysalis all the way from Arizona to Idaho.

Maybe it's because I'm social,
or maybe it's because of family reunions,
a tradition that stopped being a tradition
when my father could no longer be in the same room as
my aunt.

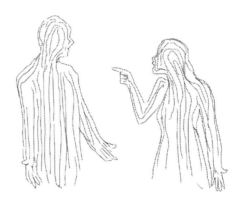

"You'll understand when you're older," they told me.
It took nearly a decade for me to be older, I guess.
I didn't hear the arguments back then;
I was too busy playing in puddles—

puddles right in front of the huckleberry pie shop,
where butterflies constellated.
I dipped my arms in the dirty water,

and butterflies landed on me.
Such delicate creatures.
I remember crying once
after lifting my shoe to find a wing
in pieces.
It takes so little to leave them in pieces,
but they still alight—
my skin, the landing zone.
So vulnerable yet trusting.

I've trusted before.

Ironically, I described his kisses as butterfly wings against my skin.

My forehead, just above the arch of my left eyebrow, my cheekbone.

My lips.

I wrote about it after the first time we had sex.

Once, I trusted a horse.
His name was Tall Tom because, well, he was tall,
measuring a great distance from bottom to top,
but the distance between him and the other horses
was always short.
He didn't like being away from the others,
and when I tried exploring on my own,
he wasn't too thrilled.
Separation anxiety; I get it.
But imagine being on top of a bucking bronco named for
its towering physique.
Pretty fucking scary.

Luckily, Grandpa came to the rescue.
I still wasn't afraid of horses after that;
the horse broke my ego,
not my heart.
Besides, it wasn't the horse's fault.
Tall Tom never tricked me into trusting.

Two years later and in the same pasture,
my grandpa protected me again.
The transgressor this time—
a motorized stallion.
I almost drove the four-wheeler off a ridge,
but he quickly backed up the tractor so I'd crash into him
instead.

This was the first motor vehicle crash I remember.
I was in another while I was still in a car seat,
but I don't remember the minivan rolling down the
mountain.
I don't remember the broken glass.
I don't remember my mother sobbing,
hand over belly,
waiting desperately for something—
a kick.
I only remember that the ambulance smelled of blood
and old people.

The second crash I remember was a practical joke made
by God,
a pretty shitty comedian.
Twenty-eight minutes after explaining to someone why I
hate the rain,
I hydroplaned on Interstate 10,
mid–acoustic version of "Take On Me" from MTV.

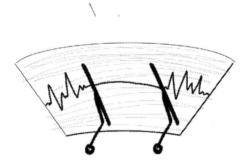

I spun across the highway,
high beams blinding me.
*Holy shit. Holy shit. I'm going to die,*
I was thinking just before I crashed into a guardrail—
not good ol' Grandad's tractor but pretty damn close.

Irony
is the passenger-side airbags inflating
but not mine.
Irony
is wanting solace
after almost dying
and calling the boy
who would finish me off a few weeks later.

Irony
is studying romanticism in philosophy class
the day after he dumped me
under the water tower, next to his work.

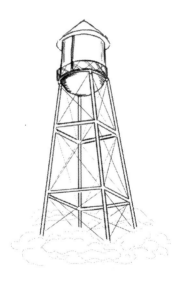

It was the typical it's-not-you-it's-me bullshit excuse—
only the oldest cliché in breakup history.
History.
That's what he made me.
But because his dad committed suicide,
it's dangerous to question the whole
I-need-to-learn-how-to-love-myself-before-I-love-
someone-else reason,
so it was easy to make me history.

It takes a creative person to make
somebody
into something then
into nothing.

Do you know what it feels like
to sit there,
crisscross, applesauce,
attempting to connect to the universe,
to speak to that son of a bitch in the sky—
that jester up above—
while everyone else scribbles their affirmations
and your sticky note is blank?

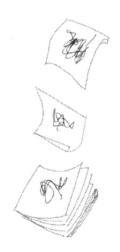

Nothing.
No answers.
The only one without answers in the meditation class.
I want to scream,

*Hello, Mr. I Don't Seem to Care!*
I do.
You once told me my eyes were your favorite color.
It took me a week to look in the mirror
and see anything other than you in them.

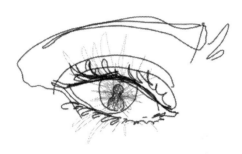

The monarch orange,
energy drinks
upon energy drinks.
The sage,
a shade of green leaning toward gray.
There's not much to say
except hazel eyes change color
when misty,
Mr. Make Up Your Mind.

It didn't take quite as long for my sheets to stop smelling like you.
At least it wasn't hard to sleep.
I slept just fine;
The problem was waking up.
That was much more painful than falling asleep.

Fun fact:
the same areas of the brain are activated
when you feel emotional and physical pain,
and often
these areas respond to emotional hurt
by increasing the activity of the vagus nerve,
which causes pain and nausea when overstimulated,
explaining terms like *heartache*,
*heartbreak*.

Heartbreak is hoping you dream about someone
despite knowing how much it'll hurt when you wake up.
You do everything in your power to hear their voice
again—
to feel them again—
even if it's all an illusion.

Once,
I dreamed of someone by accident.
I dreamed of my grandpa.
We were playing slapjack.
Usually he let me win,
but this time
I lost
when I woke up
and remembered he'd died of cancer about a month prior.

I want you to know
that I thought of you
every night
before I went to sleep
in the hope that I'd dream of you.

I want you to know
that I didn't wash the clothes you left at my house
until they stopped smelling like you,
and it took everything I had
not to return them to you
smelling like me.

I want you to know
you planted flowers
in places
I cannot water on my own.

I want you to know
that on Valentine's Day,
I bought 130 chicken nuggets.
One hundred thirty chicken nuggets.

Those chicken nuggets didn't protect me
from Scorpio this time.
Yes,
he was born in November.

My shooting star—
that's what I called him.
Something brief
and beautiful.

For Valentine's Day,
I got him a custom star map titled "Shooting Star,"
depicting the sky above us
the night I started falling for him.
Gold Canyon, Arizona; October 27, 5:39 p.m.
This star map is still in my closet.

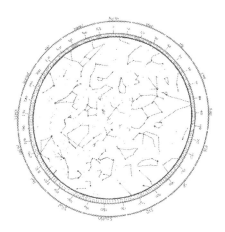

His clothes are still in my drawer.
Two pairs of sweatpants.
One blue tank top.
I can't stomach the idea of returning them.

To do so would require looking him in the eyes again,
and that's the part that's terrifying—
getting stuck in those pools of honey,
those amber saucers I fell in love with.

He may have broken up with me that Sunday under the
water tower,
but his eyes told me long before.
His fingertips told me lies
as they choreographed contemporary dances—
my skin, the marley floor—
but his eyes were much less deceitful.

I used to read them so easily.
Now, I'm afraid to.
My friends called him Weatherboy
because he is so predictable.

He lives like he's starring in a movie.
He searches for drama,
creates it,
directs it.

I was simply a character in one of his subplots.
I made it more interesting.
People love to watch a train wreck,
and I just happened to be one of the passengers.

He only wanted me because he shouldn't have.
Even forbidden fruit eventually loses its flavor,
and when it did—
when I did—
I reached my last stop.
Catch me in the credits.

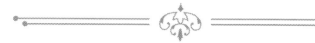

Humiliation
is grabbing two bags of Lay's barbecue potato chips, a
Gatorade, and my baby blanket
and running away at the age of seven,
only to get cold and come home after walking four blocks,
only to be disappointed my family didn't notice I was
gone.

Humiliation
is also just the opposite.
It is the first time entering his house through the front
door
instead of his bedroom window—
the first family dinner,
which went pretty well,
minus the part where his mom caught us fucking.

Humiliation
is his mom banging on the door
as I slide on my jeans and wrap up in a blanket while he
gets up to answer.
It is scrolling through my love song playlist "Butterflies,"
attempting to look busy,
because I can't make eye contact with her.

It was almost as humiliating
as jumping out of the bathroom window,
bare-ass naked,
because his parents woke up while we were in the shower.
Side note: it was cold.

Little did we know,
they knew about the sneaking around,
the climbing over walls,
the jumping through windows.
Apparently, his observant grandma isn't the best at
keeping secrets.

My grandma has a secret garden.
That's just what it's called.
It's not really a secret.

More often than not,
things we think are secrets are not really secrets at all.
I learned that in high school.

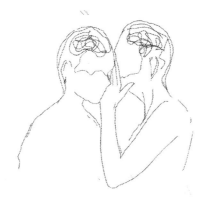

I learned a lot of things in high school, as follows:

1. Never choose the person you're dating for a science fair partner.
2. Antiderivatives make me want to blow my brains out.
3. The best place to go if you need to cry is the big stall in the back of the girls' bathroom. Nobody uses that one because the lock is broken.

The key
is not expecting someone to speak to you
in a language they don't know.
Trust that broken record.
Trust the repetition of "I don't know"
again and again and again,
and don't wait.

There's nothing quite like it.
There's nothing quite like perpetuating love
through letters and dreams
and realizing it wasn't meant to be
much later than he does.
He just didn't have the heart to tell me.

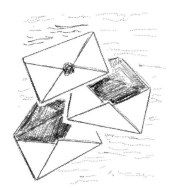

This time,
it was different.
There were no broken records,
just lies
in a language we both knew.

*Love* is an easier word than it is a language.
It's easy to say *love*
and not mean it.

I do hope, however,
that the opposite is true as well
and that people don't really mean it
when they tell me they don't.

My sister once informed me
that all the ways I show her I love her
annoy the hell out of her.
We speak different love languages, I guess,
and hers is some sort of enigma to me.
Rotors, ciphers, wheels
always turning.
I'm no Alan Turing.

I cried that night.
Hard.
Like soaked-my-jeans-from-crying-into-my-knees hard.
What people say,
good or bad,
affects me
a lot.
I think it has to do with my love language.

Over the summer,
my dad sent me a letter telling me he was proud of me.
I cried that night too.
That time, it was just a few tears.
Good tears.

It was hard being away from my family over the summer, reading updates in the form of weekly letters.
Extra! Extra!
Read all about it!

Read all about
how the second-youngest is in season 4 of *Glee*.
Read all about
how the second-oldest starred in a musical.

Read all about
how the mother cheated on the ex-stepdad
and moved into a rental house half the size of the last
with her new boyfriend,
who is still married with kids.
Let's just say family dinners are very interesting.

I condemned it then—
the cheating.
Little did I know,
I would be an instrument in a similar orchestration
just a few months later.

They say the apple doesn't fall far from the tree.
I don't know who "they" are,
but "they" must be pretty damn smart.

I want to be like them someday.
Meditative.
Not thoughtless and rash.
Not the epitome of insecurity playing masquerade.
Not somebody who buys 130 chicken nuggets
on Valentine's Day
just to scatter them around their ex's front yard
after attending "I'm Single and I'm Okay" night at Sozo's
coffeehouse.
Evidently,
I was single and very much not okay,
so when my friends asked to toilet-paper his house, I
considered it
before refusing.

I didn't want to do anything major,
just something trivial,
like leaving a fish on his doorstep,
like "*Ha*, now you have to take care of a fish!"

But the PetSmarts were closed,
and the woman at Walmart was so drunk off her ass
she forgot they sold fish.
And Burger King sells ten chicken nuggets for $1.49,
and we had a twenty-dollar bill,
so it only made sense
to buy 130 chicken nuggets and distribute them across his
lawn.

You're probably thinking,
*What were you thinking?*
The answer is simple:
I wasn't.
Maybe I just wanted to remind him I exist.
Remind him I exist.
I exist

loudly.
I can't change the volume of the voice in my head,
so I change it from the outside.
If my thoughts remain my own,
they are trees falling
in forests
with no one around to hear them.

I want them to make sounds.
I know they make sounds,
blaring, blasting, booming—
blooming in my head
like daffodils.

Never confuse a narcissist and a narcissus.
One is self-regarding.
One is self-reviving.
I choose the latter.
I choose new beginnings.
I choose to grow,
to learn,
to exist
as I am and better.

Printed in the United States
By Bookmasters